Gardening
WITH THE EXPERTS

SHADY
GARDENS

Gardening WITH THE EXPERTS

SHADY GARDENS

MARY MOODY

Bloomsbury Books
London

*Cover: A colourful mix of **azaleas** and **polyanthus**, blooming in the shade.*

Published by Harlaxton Publishing Ltd
2 Avenue Road, Grantham, Lincolnshire, NG31 6TA, United Kingdom.
A Member of the Weldon International Group of Companies.

First published in 1992.

© Copyright Harlaxton Publishing Ltd
© Copyright design Harlaxton Publishing Ltd

This edition published in 1993 by
Bloomsbury Books
an imprint of
The Godfrey Cave Group
42 Bloomsbury Street, London. WC1B 3QJ
under license from Harlaxton Publishing Ltd.

Publishing Manager: Robin Burgess
Project Coordinator: Mary Moody
Editor: Christine Mackinnon
Illustrator: Kathie Baxter Smith
Designed & produced for the publisher by Phillip Mathews Publishers
Produced in Singapore by Imago

British Library Cataloguing-in-Publication data.
A catalogue record for this book is available from the British Library.
Title: Gardening with the Experts: Shady Gardens
ISBN:1 85471 196 2

CONTENTS

INTRODUCTION

Most gardens have areas that are shady, where a canopy of established trees block direct sunlight to the undergrowth.

Some gardens, are predominantly shady, and this poses problems for those gardeners who wish to introduce colour and texture to the landscape.

Although shade is welcoming in the heat of summer, too often shady parts of the garden are bare, denuded of vegetation, making them a less-than-inviting retreat.

With some thought and planning it is easy to cultivate a fertile garden in the shade, taking into account the demands of this special environment and the types of plants that best suit the conditions.

Types of shade

Dark areas of the garden may be caused by mature trees with spreading branches, or by buildings that cast a permanent shadow on one particular patch. In hotter climates the

*Above: Even annuals such as **Ageratum** can be grown in semi-shaded conditions.*
*Opposite: **Ferns** thrive in a shady glen, surrounded by natural rock.*

Shade can be created by spreading trees, buildings, fences or walls.

shade may have been designed deliberately to cool the house, incorporating either a deep verandah or pergola covered with climbing plants.

Some areas are shaded for only a few hours of the day, while others benefit from dappled sunlight filtering through over-hanging trees, shrubs or climbers.

The way in which you approach shade gardening will depend on two major factors — the degree of shade and the soil conditions — of the area where you plan to create or develop a garden, plant a lawn or ground cover.

Beneath established trees: These areas are notoriously dry and barren because established trees generally have a thick root system that depletes the soil of moisture and nutrients.

Work will be needed to improve the soil if plants and grass are to compete in these unfavourable conditions.

Shaded by the house: Narrow pathways beside the house can look dark and dreary due to lack of sun. Yet clever gardeners will make the most of these conditions to create a lush fernery with climbers and ground covers in every nook and cranny. If the house is well positioned these spaces are fortunate to be sheltered from gusty winds, making them ideal for plants that need cool, dark and protected positions.

Dappled shade: Areas of dappled shade are more restful and soothing than full shade. So many species thrive in dappled light that it is well worth planning and planting a special bed if such an area occurs in your garden.

Most ferns love dappled shade, and this can be an ideal location for a series of hanging baskets festooned with plant colour and form.

Semi-shade: This is a term often seen in gardening books which refers to areas that are shaded for only part of the day.

There are many species that both prefer and grow better in these conditions than in either full sun or full shade.

LANDSCAPING TECHNIQUES

Finding solutions to shaded areas of the garden depends on where and how they occur. There are many landscaping techniques that will help overcome shade problems, no matter how difficult.

Beneath the trees: First consider the best and most practical use of the shaded area. The space beneath tree shade is good for creating paved casual outdoor living areas. As lawn or garden beds are more difficult to cultivate under trees, consider fixed paving as an alternative — always try to choose a natural colour and finish, to blend rather than stand out from the landscape.

Some shade trees may need lower branches trimmed to create sufficient headroom. This can also allow some natural sunlight to penetrate at times of the day, making cultivation a little easier. Very thickly branched and leaved trees can be thinned, again to create dappled light rather than deep shade. Maintain the natural shape of the tree when pruning.

When designing and planning a garden bed beneath the spread of tree shade, keep in mind that the root system of the tree may extend at least as far as the branch span. This means that extra organic matter and watering will be required over the

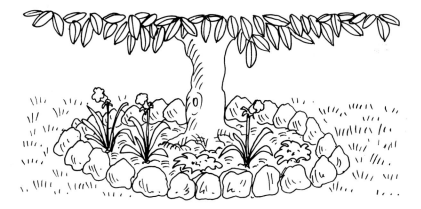

Built-up garden beds beneath trees create better growing conditions for most species.

9

whole area, not just around the tree trunk.

Consider trying to create a natural or 'naturalised effect' by scattering bulbs and suitable 'old- fashioned' plants at random. This will create a particularly good effect in spring.

Garden beds in the shade: These are generally either too dry or too damp. The dryness is the result of competition from the roots of overhanging trees and shrubs, or dampness caused by areas that receive no sunlight and have poor drainage.

In both situations, building up the soil with organic matter is the best solution. If the soil level needs to be raised more than 20cm (8in) consider building small retaining edges to hold the new soil in place. Bricks, rocks, timber sleepers, logs or terracotta edging tiles are all suitable edging materials for this purpose.

A simple spaded edge is the cheapest way of finishing a garden bed — simply mound up the organic matter in the bed and dig a neat trench around the outside. This makes mowing easier, as the mower blades can be taken right up to the spaded edge, avoiding the need for trimming with clippers.

A shaded water-garden: This solution is ideal for areas where damp shade is a problem. Create a small pond or water-garden for bog plants and other moisture-loving species, which will transform a difficult area. Such a location is an opportunity tgat lends itself visually to a pond, it should be designed to look as natural as possible — as though it had always been there!

Ferns thrive in damp shady positions, so a mixed planting of ferns alongside a small pond will look enchanting. A simple pond can be built by excavating a hole, then

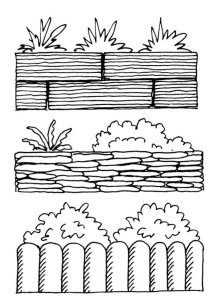

Beds can be edged with railway sleepers, rocks or terracotta edging tiles.

lining it with either thick dark plastic or other lining material designed for the purpose. More complex pond designs or those with pumped water systems, will probably require professional installation.

A shaded rock garden: This has the effect of creating good natural drainage for a range of small shade-loving species.

Boulders, rocks or stones should be positioned with care, to emulate nature. Avoid using concrete, especially visible joints. Use a rich soil mixture between rocks and boulders that will give plants a good start. Encourage moss growth on the rocks and boulders to give a more weath-ered appearance.

*A massed planting of **azalea** beneath a canopy of pines, providing exactly the right growing conditions.*

*Fallen pine needles can be used as a mulch around **azaleas** and **rhododendrons**.*

HEALTHY SOIL, HEALTHY GARDEN

Healthy soil is essential to the success of a garden in the shade. Time spent building and improving the soil will determine the health of the plants; therefore time and energy spend getting the soil just right before planting is essential.

In an existing shade garden with poor soil, work at improving conditions by adding layers of organic matter as a mulch between plants.

The first step in establishing the health of the soil is testing for the texture. Basically soils can be divided into three categories:

    (i) light and sandy
    (ii) good average loam
    (iii) heavy and clay.

Sandy soil is light and easy to cultivate, but has the disadvantage of allowing moisture to drain away too quickly after

Intensive planting is the result of healthy, rich soil.

rainfall or watering.

To adjust sandy soil, add quantities of well-rotted compost and manure to improve moisture-holding capacity.

Average loam describes soils that are neither too sandy nor too high in clay content. A good loam will hold moisture well, yet allow excess water to drain away easily. Texture improvement is generally not necessary.

Clay soils are heavy and hard to work. They take a long time to drain after rainfall, best way to correct their texture is to add lots of organic matter in the form of compost or well-rotted manure.

The second important factor in the health of the soil is its drainage quality. A simple test can determine just how good drainage is in a particular area.

First, dig a deep hole then fill it with water to the brim. Allow some time for the water to drain away. If the water does not empty at the base of the hole after an hour or so, some correction to the drainage may be needed.

Soils with high clay content are notoriously slow to drain. Correct this by simply adding lots of organic matter to the soil to improve the texture and thus the drainage.

Soils that are too light and sandy are also adjusted by the addition of compost and other organic matter.

As an alternative consider building up garden beds above ground level to create built-in drainage. Add large amounts of organic matter and use railway sleepers or stones to form an edge that will hold the soil in place. As the plants grow their roots will travel downwards into the clay, then gradually drainage will improve.

Consider compost
Home-made compost is the most useful soil additive available, and all gardeners can make their own!

Compost is made by the decomposition of organic materials. To be successful, a compost heap needs both water and air to generate heat that is required to hasten the breaking down process. If allowed to dry

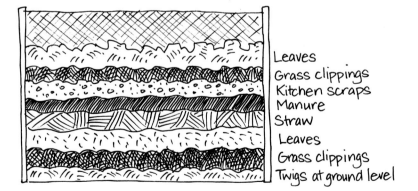

Leaves
Grass clippings
Kitchen scraps
Manure
Straw
Leaves
Grass clippings
Twigs at ground level

A healthy compost is made by layering organic materials.
Mesh sides help air and moisture to penetrate.

out the process will slow down. Likewise, if air cannot circulate throughout the compost materials the entire process will take much longer.

Water the compost every week in dry weather, then lightly turn the ingredients with a fork to allow air penetration. To speed up the process add a powdered herbal activator containing a variety of herbs including *comfrey*.

The best compost is built layer upon layer, allowing organic materials of various thicknesses and textures to break down as quickly as possible. Fine materials such as grass clippings will heat up quickly and help to activate coarser materials such as straw or shredded bark.

Try to vary layers — start with grass clippings, then add some vegetable scraps, wood ashes from the fireplace or bonfire, straw, some animal manure (poultry, cow, horse) and then leaves. Keep layering, varying ingredients as you go, until the heap is about one metre (3ft) in height.

Mulch

Mulching shady gardens is as important as mulching gardens exposed to the direct sunlight. It prevents weeds from emerging in the soil around the base of plants and keeps the soil moist between waterings. Mulching also prevents the soil surface from drying out and improves soil texture by keeping it lightly moist. If organic mulches are used they will provide a steady stream of nutrients to the plant roots. The best mulches to use are:

Compost: Home-made compost is excellent, as is mushroom compost, for a wide variety of soil types and conditions.

Manure: Horse, cow and poultry manure can be delivered in bulk or bought by the bag. Poultry manure can be a problem for some plants as it is high in nitrogen and promotes leaf rather than flower growth; however, combined with an all-purpose plant food, it does the job.

Grass clippings: Combine these with either compost or manure in layers. Used alone, clippings will not supply nutrients.

Bark: This is a terrific top layer mulch. Use it in combination with layers of organic material such as manures or compost. Pine bark is commercially available in many grades, from a very finely chopped bark to large chunks.

Leaves: During autumn and winter leaves can be raked together in a heap, then watered and allowed to break down into leaf mulch. Leaves can also be raked directly onto the garden where they will break down gradually. To prevent them from blowing away try sprinkling a layer of well-rotted manure on top. This will also hasten the decomposition process, while keeping the leaves in order.

Regular mulching and feeding will produce good results.

MAINTAINING A SHADY GARDEN

Dark areas of the garden need as much care and attention as sunnier spots. Even if weeds are less prolific, work will still be required in routine watering, weeding, mulching, feeding and fertilising to keep a shady garden healthy and blooming.

Watering

Water is a vital resource that should never be taken for granted. Gardens in shade areas still need plenty of water to compensate them for moisture lost to nearby trees and shrubs. The amount of water required by your shady garden depends on various factors.

Type of soil: Light and sandy soils dry out quickly, and therefore require more water. Heavy clay soils hold the moisture for longer but do not necessarily allow it to reach plant roots efficiently.

Garden style: An informal garden with native plants grown woodland-style needs less water than a more formal garden with neat lawns and organised garden beds.

Climate: This obviously varies enormously from region to region, with some receiving a much higher natural rainfall.

Type of shade: Areas under house eaves and alongside buildings often do not get damp even after rain. The ground beneath trees and shrubs suffers from so much competition for moisture that the ground will often appear dry shortly after watering.

Watering methods

Automatic sprinkler systems: Automatic sprinklers can be very wasteful since they encourage over-watering. Although automatic systems are time saving, great care must be taken or excess water will drain valuable soil nutrients and destroy soil texture.

Select a suitable sprinkler for each area of the garden.

Hand-held hose: This is excellent for the keen gardener who likes to keep in touch with the garden, making time to keep a regular check on plants.

In a large garden, watering by hand is probably too time consuming but an effort should be made to water at least part of the garden by hand every month, so you can examine plants as you water, looking for possible problems.

Sprinklers: There are many styles of sprinkler to choose from — ranging from those designed for watering wide sweeping lawns to those for narrow garden beds.

The choice of sprinkler type will depend on the area that needs to be watered and the water pressure where you live. Large sprinklers require good pressure to work efficiently, so if your water pressure is low choose a smaller, simpler model.

Soaker hoses and drip watering: Good for reducing water consumption, especially for areas under trees and shrubs, these direct water straight to where it is needed.

Water deeply

Encourage plant roots to travel downwards in search of moisture by watering less frequently, but deeply. This is especially important under trees and shrubs where plant roots will surface and compete with the roots of plant undergrowth.

Shallow watering encourages roots to move upwards, making plants dependent on regular watering. In general, gardens can also be encouraged to exist with less water during long dry periods if watering is decreased gradually.

When to water

Although watering times in shaded areas are less critical than in sunny spots, avoid late afternoon waterings in winter if your climate is cold, as this could turn to ice. Otherwise water when convenient, remembering always to water deeply.

Mulching

The most efficient way to reduce the garden demand for watering is by mulching well between the plants. Mulching acts as a protective layer between the soil and the elements, helping to reduce drying out and surface caking. Mulch keeps weed growth down, which prevents weeds taking moisture from the soil. It also helps to keep the soil from freezing solid during harsh winters. A garden that has been well mulched will probably require half as much water as one where the soil is exposed.

Feeding the garden

Regular feeding is an important way of keeping plants healthy, especially plants located in areas where there is competition from others for nutrients.

The general rule when feeding plants is to apply regular small doses of fertiliser, rather than concentrated doses of plant food once a year. A slow release of

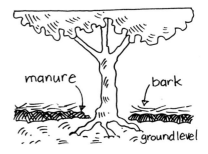

Apply mulch in layers, taking care not to place it too close to the trunk or stem of the plant.

Fallen leaves and petals can be raked and used as a mulch or as an ingredient of the compost.

nutrients will result in steady growth, with the best results.

When feeding plants make sure that the ground is lightly damp, never apply either organic or chemical fertilisers to dry soil!

Liquid plant food is an easy and efficient way to fertilise the garden. Concentrated liquid fertiliser is mixed with water in a watering can and applied to the garden as needed.

Side dressings of organic fertilisers, such as blood and bone or concentrated poultry manure pellets can be scattered at the base of plants, gradually mulching down to provide a steady stream of nutrients.

Slow release fertilisers work on the basis of releasing nutrients slowly as the ground is watered, they should be used in conjunction with some worthwhile organic mulch.

Weeding

Keeping garden beds weed free reduces problems with pests and diseases. Overgrown weeds strangle plants and compete for moisture and nutrients.

Weeding should only be done when the soil is damp, then the ground should be mulched immediately with organic matter (leaves, compost, manure, bark) to prevent weeds regrowing.

PLANTS FOR DEEP SHADE

Aucuba japonica (spotted laurel): A hardy shrub that grows between 1.5 and 2 metres (4-6ft) in height with delicately toothed deep green leaves which form a shiny backdrop for brilliant bright red berries.

Brunnera macrophylla: A perennial which has bright blue flowers in spring. Growing to 45cm (18in) in height, this easy-to-grow plant spreads quickly from seed, having attractive foliage as well as flowers.

Buxus sempervirens (English box): A hardy shrub that grows to 4.5 metres (15ft), is often used as a hedge in shady gardens. The leaves are glossy and respond well to trimming in late summer. Sometimes used for topiary.

Convallaria majalis (lily of the valley): A delightful hardy perennial which grows to 20 cm (8in) with broad, bright green leaves

Group potted plants together against a shaded wall or fence.

and delightful fragrant white bellflowers. Multiplies rapidly in the right conditions. A pink form is also available; however it is not as vigorous.

Euphorbia robbiae: A useful perennial with masses of leathery green leaves and rosettes of yellow-green flowers during spring and summer. Will grow to 60cm (2ft) in the right conditions, is tolerant of dry and moist shade. A good ground cover.

Fatsia japonica (false castor oil plant): A good plant for large pots on patios, this foliage plant has handsome leaves and creamy flowers in autumn.

Gaultheria shallon: Useful beneath trees, a hardy shrub that can be very invasive if allowed to take over. Can grow to 2 metres (6ft), with leathery leaves and attractive pink and white bellflowers and purple berries. Can be grown in both dry and damp shade.

Haberlea rhodopensis: This low growing perennial is useful as ground cover, with glossy green leaves and open, lilac flowers in spring. Can be cultivated in full shade or semi-shade, it is suited to planting in wall crevices or shady rockeries.

Hedera helix (ivy): Useful in many situations, ivy will grow in the most difficult conditions and quickly spread to cover problem areas. Many foliage forms available, from large and glossy to small and variegated.

Hydrangeas that are well watered and pruned will bloom prolifically.

Helleborus orientalis (lenten rose): A pretty old-fashioned perennial, growing to 60 cm (2ft), with attractive foliage and showy purple, pink or white flowers according to the hybrid. Perfect for a cottage garden, it can be grown in full or semi-shade.

Helleborus niger (Christmas rose): This showy perennial, grows to 45cm (18in), has masses of white flowers during late winter-early spring. Can be grown in full or semi-shade.

Helleborus corsicus (Corsican Hellebore): Another form of *heleborus*, growing to 60 cm (2ft), with tall heads of pale green flowers in late winter and early spring. Excellent for inadequate or stony soils, in either full or semi-shade.

Hydrangea macrophylla: A popular mild climate *hydrangea*, grows to 1.5 (4ft 6in) metres with large showy heads of flowers that vary in colour according to the soil conditions. Canes should be cut back after flowering. Needs a heavy watering regime in warm regions.

Hypericum calycinum (rose of Sharon): This small shrub has masses of open yellow flowers during summer through to early autumn. Useful because of its ability to adapt to a wide range of soils and conditions. Occasional pruning prevents it becoming leggy.

Iris foetidissima (Gladwyn iris): One of the few *irises* that likes shaded conditions, this species is enjoyed more for its dramatic orange-red berries than for the yellow-lilac flowers that appear in summer.

Lamium galeobdolon (yellow archangel):

This plant is inclined to take over the garden, however it certainly provides a good coverage in dark and difficult corners. Valued for its foliage, which is light green and variegated, the small yellow flowers appear in summer but are not very showy.

Lamium maculatum 'Roseum' (spotted dead nettle): This perennial grows to 25cm (10in) and has a spreading habit that is ideal for rockeries. The foliage is pale green variegated with pink, the pink flowers appear in spring and early summer.

Ligustrum japonicum (Japanese privet): A fast-growing shrub that can survive very poor conditions. The foliage is smooth and dark green, while the small white flowers bloom in summer.

Mahonia aquafolium (Oregon grape): This hardy shrub grows to 120 cm (4ft) and has glossy dark green leaves and showy panicles of flowers in spring. This species has a suckering, spreading habit that is useful as a ground cover in dark, moist situations.

Pachysandra terminalis: A groundcover shrub that is very tolerant of poor growing conditions, even under trees and large shrubs. Clusters of white tubular flowers bloom in mid-spring.

Polygonatum x hybridum (Solomon's seal): A useful hardy perennial with arching stems of foliage growing to 90cm (35in) with delicate pendulous white-green flowers in late spring. Prefers cool, moist soil, where it will quickly spread.

Ramonda myconii: A ground covering perennial with dark green leaves and open lavender flowers in spring. Ideal for cool, shady positions, with well-drained soils rich in organic matter.

Rhododendron : Although *rhododendrons* (including *azaleas*) generally prefer filtered or semi-shaded conditions, there are several species that will grow in full shade.

Most *rhododendrons* prefer cool, highland gardens, where they thrive in rich, moist soil. Consult a specialist nursery about those species that with-stand full shade.

Rubus ulmifolius: A fast-growing bramble that needs to be controlled, yet will provide a good coverage of decorative dark leaves and pretty purple-pink flowers in

A raised garden bed that gets morning sun and afternoon shade.

Glorious **rhododendron** *flowers, ideal for cool, moist gardens.*

mid-summer. Excellent for areas of shade with poor soil.

Saxifraga fortunei: A low-growing perennial with attractive foliage and tall stems of feathery white flowers in autumn. Grows best in full shade and a rich, moist soil with some protection from cold winds.

Scrophularia aquatica 'Variegata' (fig-wort): A perfect perennial for planting beside shaded streams, growing to 80cm (32in) with cream and green variegated foliage. Soil must be rich and moist for satisfactory results.

Symphytum grandiflorum: A ground-covering relative of the *comfrey* plant, this pretty perennial grows very well under trees and shrubs providing the soil is moist. Creamy flowers appear in spring.

Vinca major 'Elegantissima' (greater periwinkle): A perennial with variegated cream and green foliage with small purple-blue flowers in mid-spring to early summer. Forms a delightful carpet of foliage as it grows in shady areas.

Viola cornuta (horned violet): This is an easy-to-grow perennial, covered with a mass of flowers in spring. The soil should be rich and moist for the best results.

PLANTS FOR SEMI-SHADE

Agapanthus (African lily): One of the toughest of all plants, with dark green strap-like leaves and circular flowerheads of blue or white on tall stalks. Choose a sheltered position.

Ajuga pyramidalis: A fast-growing ground cover with attractive bronze-green foliage and small flower spikes of bright blue. Moist soil is essential. A variegated form is also available.

Arabis (rock cress): A pretty and fast-spreading ground cover with silver-grey foliage, masses of white flowers in spring. Needs a well-drained soil for best results.

Aquilegia (Columbine): A wide range of perennials, inclues some colourful hybrids, with foliage resembling maidenhair ferns, slender spikes topped by nodding flowers of mauve, crimson, pink, purple, blue, yellow and white. Moist soil is required.

Astilbe (goat's beard): A range of beautiful summer-flowering perennials with fern-like foliage and soft feathery flowers. A traditional cottage garden plant which likes a good moist soil.

Azalea: Most azaleas thrive in semi-shaded conditions, except for the 'Mollis' *azaleas* which seem to prefer more sun.

Well-drained soil and sufficient moisture are essential for good results. Mulch well around shrubs as they are shallow rooted.

Begonia: Most begonias prefer semi-shaded conditions, producing fleshy leaves and spectacular flowers during summer. Rich moist soil is necessary for good results.

Berberis darwinii (barberry): A pretty shrub with glossy leaves, clusters of orange-yellow flowers and sharp thorns, often used as an informal hedge in a shady garden.

Bergenia (pig squeak): A hardy ground

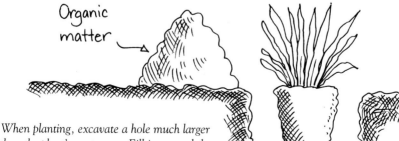

When planting, excavate a hole much larger than the plant's root mass. Fill in around the plant with rich organic matter.

Camellias sasanquas thrive in semi-shade in rich, moist soil.

covering plant with oval green leaves and rosy purple flowers in spring. Good for poorer soils.

Camellia: As *camellias* like sheltered situations, semi-shade is ideal; however some sunlight is required to produce a good flower display. Excellent as background or feature plants, camellias like rich soil and should be well mulched.

Campanula (bellflower): Many species, from ground covers to large herbaceous plants, mostly with blue, white or mauve flowers. Must have rich moist soil.

Crocus: A delightful group of spring, winter or autumn-flowering bulbs, excellent in small rock gardens, beneath shrubs or trees.

Daphne odora: A charming small shrub, growing to one metre (3ft) in height, with glossy foliage and fragrant white flowers tinged with purple. Some sun is necessary for flowering.

Dicentra spectabilis (bleeding hearts): A charming old-fashioned perennial with fern-like foliage and pink bellflowers in late spring. Suited to cool, moist positions.

Forsythia: A fast-growing spring-flowering shrub with masses of yellow flowers. Old wood should be pruned out after flowering.

Fritillaria imperialis (crown imperial): An impressive bulb with tall stems of lemon-yellow or orange-red flowers in spring. Difficult to cultivate.

Camellia flowers require protection from strong winds and harsh sunlight.

Fuchsia: A wide range of charming shrubs with drooping flowers, some very large and colourful. Cool, moist growing conditions are required for good flowering.

Hydrangea: A popular group of deciduous shrubs with massive flowerheads that vary in colour according to the soil conditions — blue in acid soils and pink where the soil is alkaline. Prune back in early spring to produce bushy growth.

Hypericum (St John's wort): A range of deciduous or semi-evergreen shrubs with showy yellow flowers over many months, from mid-summer. Prune in early spring.

Ilex aquifolium (English holly): An evergreen shrub or small tree suited to cool climates, with glossy green foliage and red berries in mid-winter.

Leucojum (snowflake): A delightful bulb that forms a clump of green strap-like leaves with delicate white bellflowers in late winter. Likes a moderately rich and moist soil.

Lupinus (lupins): A charming old-fashioned perennial with attractive foliage and flower spikes in many colours. Lupins can be grown in partial shade if rich moist soil is present.

Nandina domestica (heavenly bamboo): A compact shrub that has brightly coloured autumn foliage with attractive red berries in summer and through winter.

Narcissus: Both daffodils and jonquils like semi-shaded situations, provided that the soil is moderately rich and well drained. Ensure they remain moist, not wet, during spring growth.

Paeonia (peony): A handsome perennial for partial shade, with attractive foliage and large, showy flowerheads in a variety of colours.

Much prefers a cooler climate, but well suited to growth beneath sheltering shrubs and banks.

Philadelphus (mock orange): A delightful old-fashioned deciduous shrub growing to 2 metres (6ft), with fragrant white or creamy-white flowers in summer.

Pieris japonica: An evergreen shrub with glossy green foliage and pendulous panicles of tiny cream-white bell flowers in mid-spring. Needs a sheltered position in cooler climates.

Pittosporum tobira 'Variegatum': A hardy shrub, excellent as a hedge in sheltered gardens, with silver variegated leaves.

Potentilla fruticosa (Cinquefoil): A valuable summer-flowering shrub with grey-green foliage and showy yellow flowers.

Syringia (lilac): A cold climate deciduous shrub that reaches 1.5 metres in height with drooping sprays of lavender pink, purple or white flowers in spring.

Viburnum: A delightful group of shrubs, some deciduous, some evergreen, with scented flowers and bright green foliage. Some support clusters of berries.

Weigela florida: A graceful shrub with arching stems covered with pink flowers. Prune back after flowering.

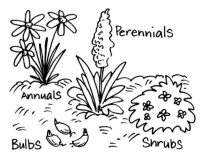

Add interest by mixing shrubs, perennials, annuals and bulbs together.

A shadehouse creates the right conditions for the cultivation of a wide range of species.

*Colourful **azalea** flowers will remain on the plant for many weeks in the right conditions.*

Soil beneath trees is generally dry, making cultivation difficult.

PLANTS FOR SEMI-DRY SHADE

Anemone nemorosa (wood anenome): This spring-flowering tuber grows to 25cm (10in) has bright green foliage with masses of open pink-white flowers. Beautiful when naturalised beneath trees in an old-fashion style garden. Prefers moisture retentive but well-drained soil.

Aucuba japonica: see page 20.

Bergenia (pig squeak): see page 24.

Convallaria majalis (lily-of-the-valley): see page 20.

Cornus canadensis (dogwood): Light green foliage with open greenish-white flowers during summer. Prefers partial to full shade, but can withstand dry soil.

Cyclamen: There are several species suited to the dry ground beneath trees and shrubs since they need shade from direct sun with shelter from wind. They thrive in well drained soil with ample organic matter.

Dicentra eximia (eastern bleeding heart): A perennial growing to 40 cm with fern-like foliage and light pink flowers over many months from spring through to autumn. Good drainage is essential, enriched with peat, leaf mould or compost.

Digitalis grandiflora (foxglove): This old-fashion perennial has tall flower spikes up to 90cm (35in) in height. Partial shade produces more summer flowers than full shade. Keep moist in summer.

Endymion nonscriptus (bluebells): A prolific flowering bulb with hardy strap-like foliage and bellflowers on 30cm tall stems. Needs moist soil.

Epimedium (Bishop's hat): Several species

Above: An automatic watering system is useful in areas of dry shade.

Hardy
Hedera helix *(ivy)*
grows surprisingly
well even in the most
deprived conditions.

Helleborus flowers even in the darkest shade.

grow well in moist sandy loam with shaded positions including *Epimedium* x *rubrum*, which has red and yellow or white flowers in spring and *Epimedium grandiflorum* 'Rose Queen', which has deeper pink flowers from late spring through summer.
Euphorbia robbiae (spurge): Dry soils will intensify plant colouring. See page 20.
Hedera helix (ivy): See page 20.

Additional watering is required on garden beds that miss natural rainfall due to overhanging eaves.

Helleborus foetidus: flowers in deep shade, can also withstand deep well-drained moist soil conditions.
Hypericum calycinum (Aaron's beard): Will tolerate dry shade but flowering is more profuse in full sun. See page 21.
Lamium (Dead nettle): Useful in shady sites, easy to grow in poor soil. See page 22,
Lunaria (honesty): A pretty self-seeding annual which reappears every spring. Lilac-purple flowers on 75cm (30in) tall spikes, followed by circular pods used for dry floral arranging. Needs light soil and semi-shade.
Melissa officinalis (lemon balm): Aromatic herb grown in well-drained soil and semi-shade, but prefers full sun. Used to flavour fruit salads, iced drinks, also in pot-pourri.
Symphoricarpus albus (snowberry): A useful shrub that grows to 2 metres (6ft), slender upright stems, small pink summer flowers, large white berries. It can be grown in difficult locations in full or semi-shade.

SHADE-LOVING CLIMBERS

Actinidia kolomikta: A slow growing climber with green-white fragrant flowers and foliage tinged with pink. Good for planting with the protection of a sunny or partly shaded wall. Does best in rich loam soil.

Akebia quinata: A deciduous climber with blue-green foliage and deep purple flowers in spring. Can be grown in a wide range of climates and soils.

Cissus antarctica (kangaroo vine): A cool greenhouse or houseplant, rapid-growing climber that clings by tendrils. It has glossy green leaves on attractive reddish stalks.

Clematis montana: This is a quick-growing climber with white flowers. Needs sun for the flowers, but the roots and base shaded from direct sunlight.

Clerodendrum splendens: This tender evergreen climber is suitable for warm and tropical areas, or greenhouse cultivation in cooler regions. It has large leathery leaves

Cover a shaded wall with a trellis, then train climbers over it.

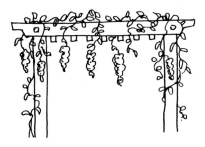

Climbers can be trained to cover archways or pergolas.

and clusters of red flowers in summer.

Hedera helix (ivy): See page 20.

Hibbertia scandens: A climber with glossy deep green foliage and open yellow flowers of unpleasant scent in summer. Needs well-drained soil. In cool regions consider pot cultivation as it requires indoor shelter.

Hoya carnosa (wax flower): A very ornamental indoor or greenhouse climber, with circular clusters of delicate pink flowers with red centres. Pretty foliage is smooth and waxy.

Jasminum primulinum (primrose jasmine): A hardy fast-growing, semi-evergreen species if sheltered by a south or south-west wall. It has tall, arching stems and yellow flowers in summer.

Lonicera caprifolium (honeysuckle);

A trellis, archway or pergola can be used for training flowering climbers.

Vigorous, invasive climber with cream or white flowers tinged with pink. Needs to have leaves in sun but root stock protected from direct sunlight. Very hardy.
Parthenocissus quinquefolia (Virginia creeper): A valuable, decidous climber with brilliant crimson autumn foliage, ideal for growing with the protection of a wall. Can be invasive if not controlled.
Stephanotis floribunda (Madagascar jasmine): This tender evergreen climber prefers warm conditions, semi-shade and a rich, moist soil. Is suited to greenhouse cultivation in cooler regions. The fragrant white flowers appear in clusters and are quite showy, much in demand by florists for button holes and bouquets.
Wisteria sinensis: A popular and showy deciduous climber, useful for semi-shaded conditions. Strong support is needed as *wisteria* can grow to quite a size after several years. Ideal in moist rich medium loam. Susceptible to frost and cold winds, therefore needs protection of a wall.

*Opposite: **Wisteria** grows well in semi-shaded areas to produce panicles of fragrant flowers.*

LAWNS FOR THE SHADE

Sometimes lawn may be the only solution to landscaping a shaded part of the garden.

While lawn requires less maintenance than a mixed flower bed, it needs regular manicuring! Regular mowing, watering and feeding, especially during spring and summer to be healthy and lush, if it is to look the part.

Warm climate grasses

In warm regions two very suitable grasses are 'Durban', and 'Buffalo', although both have a seasonal colour loss.

They also have the disadvantage of not being able to withstand heavy traffic, this makes them unsuitable for areas that will be walked upon. Also they need regular maintenance, such as mowing, watering and feeding to produce good results.

Cool climate grasses

In cool regions the scope for grass is much wider. 'Fine Fescue', 'Bent', 'Rye', 'Kentucky Bluegrass' and 'Tall Fescue' are all very shade tolerant. They will withstand wear and tear (apart from 'Bent' which is sensitive to heavy traffic).

Cool climate grasses have good colour retention throughout the year.

Lawn care

Lawns are heavy feeders, especially at the base of trees, where they will be competing for moisture and nutrients. During the main growing season (spring) a six-weekly feed of high-nitrogen lawn food will be necessary, plus regular deep watering, especially after a hot day. Shallow watering will encourage roots of surrounding trees to travel upwards in search of moisture!

Apply twice yearly top dressings of cow and poultry manure to encourage new growth and make the lawn greener.

Remember to always water the ground well before feeding the lawn — fertilisers have a tendency to burn the roots if applied to dry ground.

Help to prevent weed growth by taking care not to cut the grass too short — a height of about 5cm (2in) is ideal, this will prevent weed seeds from propagating.

Alternatives to grass

In warmer climates, instead of lawn, consider growing one of these shade-loving ground covers as a substitute: violets, *Hydrocotyle, Muehlenbeckia, Pratia* or *Marsilea augustifolia.*
Rich, moist soil is needed for good results.

*Opposite: **Violets** are an excellent alternative to lawn.*

ANNUALS FOR SEMI-SHADE

There are some annuals that can be grown successfully in semi-shaded areas, provided the soil conditions are right. In general annuals require more maintenance than perennials or climbers, but will reward the keen gardener with a colourful show of blooms if well grown.

Spring-flowering annuals are propagated by sowing of seed or planting of seedlings in autumn, while summer annuals are generally sown in early spring when the danger of frost has passed. The secret of success with annuals is to water and feed them well during the main growth period. Mulch well around the young plants when they have become established to prevent

Most annuals are grown from seedlings, which should be transplanted into well-prepared ground.

weed growth and to help maintain soil moisture. If allowed to 'go to seed' some species will reappear season after season. The following annuals are ideal for the semi-shade:

Shady annuals
Ageratum; Alyssum maritimum; Anchusa; Bergenia; Begonia semperflorens; Bellis perennis (English daisy); Browallia; Cineraria; Lobelia; Myostis (Forget-me-nots); Polyanthus; Primula; Virginia stocks.

*Pretty spring-flowering **Polyanthus**.*

*Opposite: Colourful **Bellis perennis** flower continuously through spring.*

'Mollis' azaleas thrive in
dappled shade.

CHARTS

MEDIUM SHRUBS FOR THE SHADE

Abutilon vitifolium	mauve-lavender clustered flowers: needs frost protection.
Artemisia abrotanum	aromatic silver foliage: needs sun in cool areas.
Aucuba japonica 'Variegata'	yellow speckled foliage: needs male and female for berries.
Berberis darwinii	yellow flowers, followed by blue berries: shade tolerant.
Buxus sempervirens	small, pretty leaves, tiny honey scented flowers.
Camellia japonica	many varieties: flowers easily frost damaged.
Elaeagnus pungens 'Variegata'	variegated foliage: equally suited to sun or shade.
Fatsia japonica	glossy leaves and white autumn flowers: shelter in cool areas.
Howea forsteriana	a handsome palm: needs greenhouse cultivation in cool areas.
Hydrangea macrophylla	many varieties: tender young growth easily frost damaged.
Hypericum calycinum	pretty yellow flowers: dry shade tolerant, shelter in cool areas.
Justica carnea	pink flowers: needs greenhouse cultivation in cool areas.
Leycesteria formosa	purple bracts and fruits: shade tolerant, flowers best in sun.
Luculia gratissima	fragrant pink flowers: needs cool greenhouse in cool areas, and shade from direct sunlight.
Mahonia aquifolium	attractive foliage and fragrant yellow flowers.
Myrtus communis	white flowers followed by purple ovoid fruit: greenhouse cultivate in cool areas.
Nandina domestica	elegant autumn bronze foliage: beware frost damage.
Osmanthus heterophylla	white fragrant flowers, mixed prickle and ovate foliage.
Philadelphus coronarius	orange fragrant white blossoms.
Plectranthus oertendablii	white-purple flowers: greenhouse/indoor cultivate in cool areas.
Viburnum opulus	heavy scented flowers followed by red ovoid autumn berries.
Yucca	white flower and strap foliage: needs full sun in cool areas.

In cool climates plants in **bold** need special attention.

DWARF SHRUBS FOR THE SHADE

Buxus sempervirens suffruiticosa	pretty variegated leaves, used for edging.
Cotoneaster horizontalis	herring-bone spread, red berries: prefers sun in cool areas.
Daphne laureola	glossy foliage, fragrant green-yellow flowers.
x *Fatshedera lizei*	fast-growing, glossy green leaves: flowers rare in cool areas.
Ferns (all species)	delicate foliage: suited to damp or humid shady areas.
Fuchsia magellanica	range of flower types and colours: often cut down by frost.
Hypericum calycinum	yellow flowers: flowering is more profuse in sun.
Impatiens biflora	prolific rose or yellow flowering: suited to moist shade.
Pieris japonica	young copper or aged green foliage, white bell-like flowers: suited to sheltered partial shade.
Ruscus aculeatus	for attractive red berries, plant mixed gender groups (3-5).
Skimmia japonica	cream fragrant flowers, red berries on *fragrans* (male form): needs frost protection by wall or trees.

In cool climates plants in **bold** need special attention.

Hydrangea macrophylla.

LARGE EVERGREEN SHRUBS FOR THE SHADE

Cordyline australis	strap-like foliage, up to 20' high in mild areas.
Ilex aquifolium	'festive' pleasant foliage and berries: for berries plant mixed gender groups.
Ligustrum japonicum	ovate wavy leaves, late summer tubular white flowers.
Olearia gunniana	white flowers, unusual felt underside foliage: prefers sheltered areas or coastal gardens.
Pittosporum tobira	orange fragrance cream flowers, cream and green variegated leaves: needs sheltered position in cold regions.
Prunus laurocerasus	white flowers followed by small fruit turning black.
Rhododendron ponticum	dramatic purple flowers tinged with pink.
Viburnum titnus	white -pink budded flowers: needs full sun in cool regions.

In cool climates plants in **bold** need special attention.

PRETTY PERENNIALS FOR THE SHADE

Acanthus	handsome foliage, bold flower spikes: needs deep-drained soil.
Agapanthus inapertus	strap-like leaves, circular deep blue to violet flower-heads: needs shelter from frost pockets.
Ajuga reptans	ground covering coloured foliage, bluish flower spikes.
Bergenia various and hybrids	leathery leaves, pink spring flowers in shade.
Campanula	many varieties, blue/purple flowers in sun or shade.
Chlorophytum	green and cream variegated foliage: needs well lit, draught free greenhouse/indoor cultivation in cool regions.
Clivia	strap-like foliage, orange trumpet flowers: needs greenhouse or conservatory cultivation in cool regions.
Cymbalaria muralis	carpet foliage, cream and mauve flowers: thrives in wall and rock crevices.
Helleborus foetidus	yellow-green pink rimmed flowers: needs moist soil.
Houstania caerulea	ground cover, tiny blue flowers: suits north face, moist soil.
Impatiens	many flower colours: greenhouse cultivate in cool regions.
Iris (monocotyledon)	various colours: in cool regions cultivate in full sun.
Liriope muscari	attractive foliage, violet flowers: drought resistant.
Maurandia	ivy-like foliage, violet bell flowers: needs greenhouse cultivation in cool regions.
Pachysandra terminalis	showy flower spikes, white tinged with purple.
Primula clarkei	showy rose-pink flowers: needs well-drained shaded soil.

INDEX

47